IT'S A WONDERFUL MID-LIFE CRISIS

or

THE GAY DISRUPTOR

by
Mark Nicholls

This first edition published in Australia in 2019 by:

Prahran Publishing
P.O. Box 2041, Prahran, Victoria, 3181

© Copyright Mark Nicholls 2019

Mark Nicholls has asserted his legal and moral right under the Copyright Act 1968 to be identified as the author of this work.

Published by arrangement with
Prahran Publishing, Australia.

All rights are strictly reserved.

No part of this publication may be reproduced, stored in a retrieval system or transmitted, in any form or by any other means, without the publisher's prior permission in writing. Copying of this script for performance reasons is also strictly prohibited by law, either in whole or excerpts from.

This book is sold subject to the condition that it shall not, by way of trade or otherwise, be lent, resold, hired out or otherwise circulated without the publisher's prior consent in any form of binding or cover other than that in which it is published and without similar condition, including this condition, being imposed on the subsequent purchaser.

Every reasonable effort has been made to trace copyright holders of material reproduced in this book, but if any have been inadvertently overlooked the publishers would be glad to hear from them. The story, all names, characters, and incidents portrayed in this book are fictitious. No identification with actual persons past or present, places, buildings, and products is intended or should be inferred.

ISBN 978-1-922263-12-4 Paperback
ISBN 978-1-922263-13-1 eBook

Dewey: 822.4

A catalogue record for this book is available from the National Library of Australia

Performance Licensing and Royalty Payments

Mark Nicholls retains control of both the amateur and professional stage performance rights of this play. No unauthorised performance should occur without the express and written permission of the playwright.

Restriction of Alteration

There shall be no modifications of any kind to the play including deletion of dialogue (including objectionable language), changes to characters gender or names, title of the play or music without the express and written permission from the author.

Sound and Video Recordings

This play may contain stage directions to include the use of music, video or other sound recordings either in part or in whole. The author and the publisher have not sought the right to use such content and performance rights permission should be obtained seperately. Permission to record audio and video recordings of all performances must also be explicitly given by the author in writing.

Author Credit

Performance rights approval requires credit be given to Mark Nicholls as the sole and exclusive author of the play. This obligation applies to the title page of every program or other advertising material distributed in connection to this play. The author's credit should appear immediately under the title of the play on all published material, and alongside no other individual. Font size of credit cannot be less than 50% of the largest letter used in the play's title.

Please email info@prahran.press
for all performance enquiries.

DEDICATION

for Carlo Nicholls

ABOUT THE PLAYWRIGHT

MARK NICHOLLS has been performing on various Melbourne stages since the age of six and has an extensive list of credits as a playwright, composer, singer, actor, producer and director. He is Senior Lecturer in Cinema Studies at the University of Melbourne where he has taught film since 1993.

He is the author of *Lost Objects of Desire: The Performances of Jeremy Irons* (2012), *Scorsese's Men: Melancholia and the Mob* (2004) and recently published articles on Italian Cinema, Powell and Pressburger's *The Red Shoes* and Sergei Diaghilev's celebrated company, The Ballets Russes.

Mark is a film critic and worked for many years on ABC Radio and for *The Age* newspaper, for which he wrote a weekly column between 2007 and 2009.

He lives in Melbourne with his partner, Ali Wirtz, and their two sons Oscar and Carlo.

SERIES PREFACE

I wrote these plays for only one reason, to perform them. I publish them here, therefore, somewhat reluctantly. They were never written to be read on the page by anyone but a treasured posy of performers that I trust to help me rescue them from it. They were certainly never conceived of as works of anything so respectable as literature. Nevertheless, I have found two reasons to overcome my reluctance and my usual roguish prejudice against readers and writers in favour of performers and punters. One reason is that putting these plays into print provides the opportunity for the most engaged of those who saw and heard them to revive and revise the experience. The other reason is archival. I wish to leave a permanent, if inadequate, record of the facts of their production over a decade, in a private space in Melbourne, for the benefit of both a small, dedicated paying audience, and for a smaller band of compulsive show-folk.

Writing these plays for the talented actors, musicians and backstage characters whose creations are recorded here, and having the privilege of working with these artists to produce them, has been the most satisfying occupation of my otherwise horrendously charmed and fascinating life.

Now that they have had their blessed release in print, these plays are beyond the concern of any motivation I had to write them. Read them, o curious one, and work it out for yourself! One motivation I will record, however, rests in the inspiration generously given by those who worked on and attended these cosy performances, and so brought their privileged, fleeting moments of theatre securely into being.

ABOUT THE PLAY

I began this play many years before I could find the courage to finish it. During the initial phase of writing, as I plunged Marion further and further into her own narcissism, I started to feel sorry for her partner and the kids. Certainly, for anyone with overwhelming responsibilities, there is something irresistible about the idea of chucking it all in, going AWOL and seeing who cares about it. It's a bit like turning up to your own funeral. I don't remember having any specific inclinations of my own towards this course of action. But we all we all flirt with the idea of 'Letting Go', as Paul McCartney and Wings sang it in the seventies. I probably felt this sort of thing was all just a little too attractive to pursue, even on the safety and obscurity of the page. For years, therefore, I couldn't bring myself to finish what seemed destined to result in an inevitable and painful separation for Marion and the familial, social or professional ensembles that claim her as member.

My concern for this must have abated, or my frustrations with group social life had increased, because when I returned to the play in 2017, I pursued it to the end, easily and with a guilty feeling of relish. I managed to save the family, which gave a degree of emotional cover. Jettisoning civility in Marion's professional life and in some of her extra familial social contexts, however, still seems somewhat controversial. 'Compartmentalising' seems to be what it is all about. I may be guilty of it myself, but the idea of living life playing the part of Shakespeare's Richard Gloucester (later Richard III) ("I can smile, and murder whiles I smile") remains appalling to me. Nevertheless, I am more than ever convinced that this type of interpersonal performance is not only rife, but that it is the pattern of behaviour in most professional contexts and too many personal relationships.

Thinking about Marion in this context, I was able to convince myself that I had found my much-desired happy ending. What was a horror story turned into something of a comedy – at least this is how the audience seemed to receive it in performance. It now reads as a kind of love letter to all those Maybots, Kool-Aid drinkers and professional hypocrites we encounter so regularly in life. It may be a fantasy, but I have partly fallen in love with this lot. In the age of rampant social media profiles and digital footprints, they seem to have found the secret to holding onto something of a private life.

CHARACTERS

MARION: a fifty-something-year-old, an English Literature school teacher,

MAX: a fiftyish-year-old, a pianist.

SETTING

Here and now.

It's A Wonderful Midlife Crisis was first performed at Rear 4, Clifton Hill, Victoria on the 14th of June 2018 with the following cast:

Max: Mark Nicholls

Marion: Madeleine Swain

Director: Mark Nicholls

Stage Manager: Carlo Nicholls

Assistant Stage Manager: Oscar Wirtz

Co Producer: Alison Wirtz

SCENE ONE

MAX is sitting on a sofa reading. In due course he addresses the audience.

MAX: I've known Marion for twenty-five years. Our friendship is the most – what should I say? – the most perfect that I enjoy. I think we understand the basic settings of each other's lives. So I can easily go for six months without seeing her. Then, when I do, very little of what she has to say surprises me. I know none of the details. We rarely exchange the superfluous. But whatever the topic of conversation, comprehension is fluent and re-experiencing her is always exhilarating. I am in awe of her. I admire her. I respect her. I trust her. I wait, patiently but longingly for our next meeting. "Patiently but longingly" – is that a contradiction? Whether it is or not, that's what I do. As I say, our friendship is the most perfect that I enjoy. *[He looks at his phone as MARION enters and stands beside him looking at the audience]* Then, yesterday I got this ambiguously punctuated text.

MARION: Separated Alex amicably children sent on their way happily contemplating suicide wine time?

MAX: Amusing and not atypical. But then I wondered. Was that...

MARION: Separated Alex amicably. Children sent on their way. Happily contemplating suicide. Wine time?

MAX: Or...

MARION: Separated Alex amicably. Children sent on their way happily. Contemplating suicide at wine time.

MAX: The question mark being merely a slip of the texting thumb or a studied symbol denoting an unconscious desire for approval. Or even...

MARION: "Separated. Alex amicably...

MAX: No. This could go on forever. Let's just say, I became – concerned. *[To MARION]* So what was it? Give me the details.

MARION: You don't like the details.

MAX: That is not true. It's not that I don't like the details. You don't offer them and I don't miss them. That's very different. I don't seek them out in the name of politeness. And I don't do the 'So how are Alex and the kids?' thing as a way to send Alex a message – or you for that matter – a message that I care. As I say, you don't offer and I reciprocate.

MARION: So now you want the details?

MAX: Are we having our first fundamental experience of mutual dissatisfaction? Or has it been going on for ages and I have been too stupid to notice? Have you been waiting all these years for me to ply you with questions about Alex and your love life and your kids and your job, only to spring it on me now, in the middle of my second mid-life crisis, when I am least equipped to deal with it?

MARION: I suppose not. When you think about it, this is what we do, isn't it? We see each other about once every six months, spend a long lunch hour discussing the nature of friendship or the situation in Kabul, before we rush off and then repeat the process six months later.

MAX: Perhaps it is time we did some details. Go ahead. "You honour me by anything you say to me."

MARION: Alex and I are separating. The kids are moving out and I do want a glass of wine.

MAX: And the happy contemplation of suicide?

MARION: Happy and merely contemplative.

MAX: Aha. You had better sit down.

MARION: And the glass of wine?

MAX: In due time. *[Pause]* Are you OK?

MARION: Yes. I just want a glass of wine.

MAX: That will have to wait. Tell me what's happening.

MARION: It's fine. There's nothing vicious going on. No one's sick, nobody died. I'm quite well. If that's what you mean?

MAX: You're sure?

MARION: Perfectly.

MAX: And the others are fine?

MARION: All fine and dandy.

MAX: OK. If you say so.

MARION: So, the wine?

MAX: Why not? You'd better get it. I think I need a minute.

MARION: *[Getting up]* In the fridge, yeah?

MAX: It is.

MARION gets it and pours them both a big one.

MARION: Are you all right?

MAX: I think so. But you're going to explain a bit more, I hope?

MARION: More details? This is a big day.

MAX: Previous certainties seem to be unravelling.

MARION: Good. I approve of that.

MAX: Yes. I suppose so.

SCENE 1

MARION: You are probably going to think I am mad, or that I have a fatal illness, or that there is something that either I'm not telling you or don't really understand myself. But none of those things is true, so try hard not to think that any of them may be true.

MAX: I'll try. But I am only willing to concede the second point – and maybe the third.

MARION: Hang on. Which was which? I have forgotten already.

MAX: I believe you on the illness point and maybe on the withholding point. But I am not promising anything on the matters of insanity and self-delusion.

MARION: OK. I will accept that.

MAX: Good. Go on then.

MARION: It started about six months ago. *[Interrupting herself]* Actually, I also have to add that apart from you, Alex and the kids I haven't discussed this with anyone.

MAX: I'm touched. But why do I need to know that?

MARION: It's part of my point – so far as I have one. I have been on this *[looking for the word]* 'path' for about six months. Nobody at school has said anything about it. Not one of my friends has asked, and those who seem to have some idea have accepted the situation with a frankly disturbing level of equanimity.

MAX: You mean you're shocked that they're not shocked?

MARION: I'm not shocked. I've just noted it.

MAX: OK. Keep going. I'll try to be at least *[pause]* interested. Six months ago...

MARION: Six months ago – I can't remember where I was – but it dawned on me that my life was almost entirely defined in relation to other people... and one or two things. I get up in the morning because Alex and the kids need me to do things for them. Sometimes they also want me to do things with them. Part of all that getting up business is also about turning up to work, so that I can get paid. The school needs me to do that too, the students need me and the parents also need me. I can fantasise about going to the gym or reading the paper as being 'me time' but, in the end, I really can't get away from the idea that all that stuff is also just about servicing the people and the things that I began with.

MAX: You're just realising this now?

MARION: No. I have always known it. It is just that now I am beginning to feel the full impact of its significance.

MAX: So, there is nothing you do that is in anyway – selfish.

MARION: I wouldn't say that. There has to be some part of being needed that amounts to a little selfishness.

MAX: But you wouldn't say you have anything in your life that is just about you?

MARION: That's right.

MAX: You may be right. In fact, you may be right about all of us.

MARION: Exactly. And that is fine. I love them, Alex and the kids, and the students too. I want to do things for them. It's just that what occurred to me was that I can't stand the idea that these people and these things are what appear to define my life. In fact, I refuse to believe that they do. A woman came up to me at the year seven cocktail party last year and told me, in the bluntest possible fashion, that she 'wanted me'.

MAX: You mean to teach her kid?

MARION: No, for sex! Although funnily enough they do sometimes put it that way when they want their kid in your English class. Anyway, why, I thought? She said that she thought I was a great teacher, the kids love me and that she really enjoyed my book. I was absolutely brilliant that night too, you know in really great form, and in ways that would totally baffle any KPI measures you can possibly imagine. But when I mentioned one or two of them to her she said she hadn't really noticed.

MAX: She was right to do that. I've seen you in top flight. Sex is the only possible thing she could have offered you in response.

MARION: Oh, I know. I'm amazing. Everybody wants me because they all imagine that it will rub off on them.

MAX: But it's not the 'real you'. You want to be loved for the 'essential Marion.'

MARION: No. It is the real me. How could it be anyone, or anything else? I've had fifty years to slip into character and now I am thoroughly consistent and obliging. I know my lines and, more importantly, I know my cues. Also, I know everyone else's lines and I can feed them accordingly.

MAX: So now you want to be bad Marion?

MARION: No. I want to be 'inessential' Marion. "Love on my terms, Jedediah."

MAX: *Citizen Kane*! 'And those terms are never like anybody else's.'

MARION: Because they are no one else's! They're my terms. And they're not pleas for attention. This isn't a year eleven formal. I'm not running across the room in tears so that all my little friends will come rushing after me to see what's the matter.

MAX: And to see if your boyfriend is now available

MARION: Right. But that second bit is not *Citizen Kane* it's Advise and Consent.

MAX: What about Alex and the kids? How do your terms affect them?

MARION: We were having dinner one night at home. It had been a lovely day, just a week before Christmas when all the parties stop and you can relax and just enjoy putting up the tree and reciprocating Christmas cards. I told them that I had had the most disturbing revelation that the substance of our various relationships is really not much more than mutual reliance. That we love each other, but that there is simply no way to really know that, beyond what we need from each other.

MAX: How did they respond?

MARION: Without dissent. Alex answered a text message. Cara starts telling me about soccer practice and Ollie just complained about the spaghetti sauce. Apparently, I wasn't telling them anything they didn't already know, and accept, as the norm.

MAX: How reassuring. So where did you go from there?

MARION: I suggested we sue each other for damages.

MAX: Like The Beatles!

MARION: Protect each other from the dangers of the world, so far as we can, and go our separate ways.

MAX: What? And never see each other again?

MARION: Not necessarily. Just not according to our familiar functions. Cara and Ollie have their own lives. They won't suffer financially. Alex has so much going on in her life. She will be fine. Besides if she wants me she can always find me. The kids too. It's just that the intention is to strip away all the need.

MAX: A divestment strategy!

MARION: I'm leaving work too. I've finished all my writing obligations. By this time next year I will have nothing required by or owing to anyone or anything.

MAX: What happens then?

MARION: I don't know. I'll sit quietly and preserve myself. I really hope that is when my life will begin. When I come to understand what I am rather than what I provide. More to the point, what I need. I have come so far from myself that I can't see what my needs really are. I am sure I have them. It's just that the single question I really fear at the moment is the question of what I need. It's bad enough when someone else asks me, but I ask myself the same question every day and I just can't seem to answer it. That's what I find so frightening.

MAX: Don't you think the whole exercise will simply confirm that you are the object of need?

MARION: It depends how useful I am to everyone – without all the stuff.

MAX: I doubt the others are as dispassionate about this as you suggest. They must have been terribly hurt. I don't care how self-

	involved you think they are. They're not simply beneficiaries waiting about for you to distribute the regular largesse.
MARION:	I have explained it to them very clearly. I made sure they understood and accepted my decision. Besides, if you love someone can you really refuse this kind of request? Beyond that I can't do anything for them. You see that, don't you? In a way it's precisely the point.
MAX:	It's a radical experiment. I think you are trying to bring about the end of the world. You want to sit there alone in the hours before the Sun engulfs the Earth, when you can do nothing for anyone and no one can do anything for you. Then you want to see who calls over – or at least who sends you a text message.
MARION:	And what they really want! Perhaps that explains that little kid at the year eleven formal? *[Pause]* But I also want to know what it feels like. When I am nothing more than a bug among bugs waiting to be stepped on. Does that feel lonely? Is it frightening? Will I reach out to try and help others? Will I try to pretend I know what is really happening and then tell all the other bugs that it will be all right? Or will I just sit there, quite content to let it all come down around me? I have no idea really. But I suspect that is the point when I will come to some level of understanding.

End Scene.

SCENE TWO

MARION is addressing a group of school parents.

MARION:

Come in, sit down, find your places everyone,
Take a seat, take a chair, doesn't matter where.
This is 'English 3/4', my name is Dr Hockenheimer,
Don't tease, sit up straight, stop pulling that girl's hair.
This term we do National Curriculum,
Plain English, clear thinking, Thack'ray *Van'ty Fair*,
Inspiration, freedom speech, multimedia story-telling,
Not pretty, not great, at best you'd say it's 'there'.
I've spoken to you before Sarah Smithers,
What on Earth do you think you are doing here?
You want the remedial room with Mrs Oppenheimer.
Report back to me about this time next year.
Yes, I think a tutor is a good idea.
No, a pompous uni graduate is not.
You'll just fill you head with lots of obscure and abstract theory,
Post this, post that, unadulterated rot.
All right, settle down, yes what's your question dear?
In terms of homework how much can you expect?
Five hours nightly and seven on weekends is about right
Clock-watching slackness is easy to detect.
What's that dear? Can you ask the kids to help you?
Any other good avenues of support?
Don't bother them, my love, I think you'll find them far too busy.
All those formals, parties and compuls'ry sport.
I know you find it somewhat overwhelming,
The struggle can eas'ly bring you to your knees.
What is your role? What is your job?
How can you best contribute?
Work hard, stay alive and pay the bloody fees.

End Scene.

SCENE THREE

MAX enters, removes his winter hat and coat and addresses the audience.

MAX: Six months passed until we talked again. For what it's worth, that was nothing to me. You might think it odd that someone would tell me so much, share such an intimacy with me, and then go silent. But I don't find it odd at all. It happens to me all the time. I must have that type of personality. People share their most precious secrets with me then disappear into the interior. Marion and I can go for a year without noticing it. Time flies. But I was keen to hear what had happened. There was so much at stake. She had raised all sorts of issues that were, frankly, disturbing and I was thinking about them from time to time. There was also the more comforting idea that she was just nuts. *[MARION has entered]* So how are Alex and the kids?

MARION: Are you all right?

MAX: Yes. What do you mean?

MARION: You are asking about Alex and the kids.

MAX: No. I am really asking.

MARION: No you are not. When people ask 'How's Alex?' they always mean 'Are you two still having sex?' When people ask 'How are the kids?' they really mean 'Have you managed to kill them off yet?'

MAX: I ain't people.

MARION: Which makes the question all the more weird. This new mania you have for detail is quite unnerving. I've spoken to you about it before. That's *Singin' in The Rain* right?

MAX: Lina Lamont. Stop the comic delay. What is going on with the grand experiment?

MARION: What do you mean?

MAX: You and the family and the divestment strategy?

MARION: What?

MAX: You know all your plans about stripping back.

MARION: They sound like your plans. I have been dealing with a family break-up. I don't make plans.

MAX: So the experiment is off?

MARION: You really can be quite perverse at times.

MAX: Last time I saw you, you distinctly told me all this stuff about offloading Alex and the kids and work and trying to find out what it is to be 'inessential Marion'.

MARION: Rubbish.

MAX: You did.

MARION: I didn't. Did I?

MAX: You certainly did.

MARION: That's sick. Why would I want to do that?

MAX: As a matter of fact, it sounded chillingly reasonable to me. Honestly Marion, you do need to work on your consistency. You're like Betty Draper in *Mad Men*. You seem to be a different character in every episode.

MARION: Why? You're not a TV audience. Alex and I and the kids are going through a terrible time and you want consistency. Why do you need consistency?

MAX: I suppose I don't really. So, in any case, what's going on? What's all this about a family break-up?

MARION: Well, about six months ago, as soon as Cara finished school, she and Ollie decided to get a house together and move out.

MAX: Great.

MARION: That's what I thought. It was lovely to see them doing something together. Time for the 'me tree' and more time for the 'Alex and me tree' – fantastic. The kids weren't going to be that far away and we were looking forward to some space in our lives. We packed them off to our rental in Collingwood, filled their 'fridge with food and cashed them up for at least a month, then we came home and fell asleep in the middle of trying to read the weekend

	papers for the first time in twenty years. I can't believe how right wing *The Australian* has become.
MAX:	Bliss. I mean about the empty nest, not *The Australian*.
MARION:	That's what I thought. Anyway, a few hours later we woke up, got off the couch, sat down to dinner, finished off the red, then Alex calmly announced that she's fallen in love with some leadership consultant called Kelly and that she's moving out on Monday afternoon. On my day off!
MAX:	Why?
MARION:	I suppose she thought I would be around to help her with her stuff.
MAX:	Don't try that one. Why was she moving out?
MARION:	She said she was in love with someone else. That's what people generally do, don't they?
MAX:	I don't. But what about all this love business?
MARION:	What answer could possibly satisfy that question? Does anyone know why they fall in love?
MAX:	Most people certainly think they do.
MARION:	Yeah, well in my experience their friends usually don't have a clue. Let alone their partners.

SCENE 3

MAX: So, what happened?

MARION: The next Monday she moved out.

MAX: So that was it? She didn't offer any sort of explanation?

MARION: She's in love. What could she say?

MAX: 'Sorry', I suppose?

MARION: She did say that.

MAX: I would have thought she'd offer you a bit more than 'Sorry'.

MARION: I suppose I didn't really interrogate her.

MAX: So you take Kelly and all the love nonsense at face value, do you?

MARION: I do. It's not pleasant, but I do.

MAX: God, Marion, you have this disturbing tendency to take people at their word.

MARION: Why disturbing?

MAX: Because the world doesn't work like that. You are upsetting the equilibrium.

MARION: Well, I never really take people at their word, as a matter of fact. I just firmly believe that it's not my business to deprive people of their precious illusions.

MAX: That would have to be the most selfish thing I think I have ever heard you say.

MARION: Not at all. I don't know what world you are living in, but illusions are all that most of us have to live on. It's hard enough hanging onto them myself. I'm not going around tossing them overboard for everyone else.

MAX: Fair enough, I suppose. So what happened then?

MARION: Nothing much. Stillness ensued. *[Pause]* I wandered around in a daze for a few weeks. Eventually I woke up out of it. Then I checked things around the house and at work, just to see if I had done anything odd, but I found that things were never better. You know, all the staff leave requests were done and in my sleepwalking state I had somehow managed to clean those windows and get that sad-looking balloon off the ledge that had been there since my fortieth.

MAX: What did that feel like?

MARION: It is amazing how good it feels to do those annoying jobs that sit waiting for two years.

MAX: Or ten years, in the case of the sad-looking balloon.

MARION: Yes.

MAX: Nevertheless, that particular experience of euphoria must have faded away pretty quickly.

MARION: It did.

MAX: What replaced it?

MARION: I was in the middle of cleaning out the cupboards and I stopped and thought, 'What's the point?' Then I just felt exhausted and terribly unhappy.

MAX: So, what did you do?

MARION: Nothing. Absolutely nothing.

MAX: Not even work?

MARION: No, work was fine. In fact, it is more than fine. I just keep going in every day and they keep upping my salary with a generously disproportionate level of authority and responsibility.

MAX: You must be getting tough.

MARION: Actually, I did notice I was starting to become terribly rude and nasty at school. You know, screaming at the administrators and insulting younger staff members in meetings, that sort of thing. That's treating work colleagues with the familiarity/contempt that is usually reserved for family I suspect. But then I had to stop it because I was enjoying myself far too much.

MAX: And they couldn't promote you any higher! Yes, admirable restraint. So much for school hijinks, what about the rest of your time?

MARION: It is the rest of the time that I can't really account for. I don't feel busy, I even feel a bit bored, but I just can't see where it all goes.

MAX: Bombarded by kid requests and friends and well-wishers no doubt.

MARION: Not at all. In fact, for months I have been quite alone. The phone doesn't ring. No one calls over. Do you know that during the last six months the only contact I have had with any of my friends has been initiated by me.

MAX: But who's counting?

MARION: I am now. In fact, when I think about it, it's always been the case. Don't get me wrong. I love it. My time is my own. I see who I want to see when I want to see them. When I do see my friends, I arrange it. Then we spend hours over lunch and they always say 'I love spending time with you... We have such good conversations... I'm so terrible at keeping in contact.' And then I never hear from them for a year until I feel like it, arrange to meet and the whole process is repeated all over again.

MAX: Lucky you. Friendship on demand.

MARION: I know! But it does get a bit disturbing when I remember that it doesn't happen unless I make it happen.

MAX: You should consider yourself lucky that you have that luxury.

MARION: I know I should, but I don't.

SCENE 3

MAX: It's all relative I suppose.

MARION: That's a nice way of accounting for greed and insatiability. But it doesn't really matter. I place great value on my friendships and on conversation, but I rarely find them to be enduringly insightful. At least not these days. They are pleasant and they pass the time, but the more I pursue them the more I find them to be something of a distraction.

MAX: So no harm no foul! Why do we appropriate these American sporting metaphors? It probably means something totally different to what I think it does.

MARION: No harm if you don't care about the nature of friendship.

MAX: I mean no big deal. First world problem.

MARION: Well, that is the world I live in. But you are right, in a way.

MAX: But then again there is Alex and the kids. I am still thinking they must be terribly concerned.

MARION: Oh that's all sorted. They are all back with me.

MAX: I thought you said you were dealing with a family break-up?

MARION: I am. Although I suppose you would call it family break-up once repaired. Family break-up gone horribly wrong. But I am still dealing with it. Once it has happened it doesn't actually go away.

MAX: So, they came crawling back on their hands and needs?

MARION: Not initially. Ha. That's quite good. No, not initially. They all called me and it was all very civilised, but they never asked to come home.

MAX: How did that make you feel?

MARION: Lonely. The compulsion towards company became very strong.

MAX: So, what did you do about that? I notice you never ring me at these moments.

MARION: Did I ever tell you about the woman at the year eleven cocktail party?

MAX: Who only wanted you for sex and not for your mind?

MARION: Yeah, well that's what I did.

MAX: And how did that work out?

MARION: Predictably disappointingly. She just wanted a different version of what she already had.

MAX: Remember this is what you wanted

MARION: I don't remember, as a matter of fact. But it doesn't really matter, because it was all sorted.

MAX: How?

MARION: By me, of course. I always do the directing. As it turned out the kids were floundering, but they just never asked to come back. Alex only lasted with her love romance for about a month and ever since that she has just been sitting about all alone and depressed, but again, not asking for anything. When I suggested they all just come home, they all jumped at it.

MAX: That must have been gratifying?

MARION: It was certainly bizarre. But why didn't they just say what they wanted? Why did I have to do the asking? If I don't ask, do we all just sit around, miserable and waiting for the phone that never rings?

MAX: Phones don't ring anymore, they buzz. Perhaps they wanted to prove to you that they really do only want the inessential Marion?

MARION: They never said so.

MAX: Some people find it hard to ask for the immaterial.

MARION: They shouldn't. It costs much less.

End Scene.

ENTR'ACTE

MAX (SINGS)

I've begun inspecting stamp collecting
I'm learning languages old and new,
My garden's now a berth for every plant and flower on Earth
I'm taking courses in cheese and wine appreciation too.
I'm digitising my old love letters
I've invented a new game,
I've tried my hand at writing songs for a band
Which the critics dismissed as 'tame'.
I'm looking out for action
Or at least some new distraction, 'cause
I've tried everything from soup to nuts
And I've ended up with you.
I said 'no' to that *MasterChef* cooking show
The ALP can win the next election without me,
It's really not much use putting your head within the noose
For this or that pastime or hobby.
I'm actively seeking diversion
Or some appropriate perversion, 'cause
I've tried everything from soup to nuts
And I've ended up with you.
I've given up on relying
On chocolate and impulse buying, 'cause
I've tried everything from soup to nuts
And I've ended up with you.
I've done everything from soup to nuts
And I've ended up with you.

End Entr'Acte.

SCENE FOUR

MARION sits on a sofa reading. When MAX enters she does not look up.

MAX: Six months no contact. Why not?

MARION: I don't have anything to say.

MAX: How are Alex and the kids?

MARION: They are free.

MAX: Tell me what happened.

MARION: Everyone is fine.

MAX: Tell me all about it.

MARION: I have no account to make. Nothing to explain. No desire to tell any story.

MAX: So the divestment strategy?

MARION: Is complete.

MAX: You are on your own?

MARION: Completely.

MAX: Tell me about it?

MARION: Why?

MAX: Don't you want to talk about it?

MARION: No. I am fine. I have nothing to say. I am completely satisfied in my life. I don't need to talk about it. It is my life and I am simply living it. It is not a narrative. It doesn't need to be told.

MAX: And Alex and the kids?

MARION: You're not interested in them, not really?

MAX: I am beginning to think that may, in fact, be more you than me.

MARION: Do you think so? Anyway, it doesn't matter. If you want to know about Alex and the kids, call them. For now, with me, you have any other topic of discussion you want, without the bother of the details.

MAX: So, what are you doing now?

MARION: Dull. Dull. Dull. That now comes under the heading of 'the details'. Go on, ask me about Kabul or the East-West Link. We can talk about TV shows or films if you like.

MAX: Come off it. No. You said anything other than Alex and the kids. Tell me what you are doing?

MARION: Nothing. I do nothing. I am nothing. At least nothing of any consequence.

MAX: You must be doing something?

MARION: Why? I bet plenty of people do nothing. I mean nothing that would be of any interest to you. I just go on.

SCENE 4

MAX: I think TS Eliot said that this is what *Hamlet* really should be like.

MARION: The play? 'Shakespeare's *Hamlet*, colon, The Dead Codfish Version'

MAX: I thought that was the version we usually get?

MARION: If you're lucky, although it's not the one that TS Eliot likes – too much excitement. But no, compared to my life, 'Shakespeare's *Hamlet*, colon, The Dead Codfish Version', at least, is a riot.

MAX: Are you bored?

MARION: Not at all. It's just that my life is now so simple that I have nothing even to bother withholding. All that I am is what you see and all that I can say is what you hear. With *Hamlet* at least you get an occasional manifestation of hysteria.

MAX: At least in the Dead Codfish version.

MARION: I think that is a fair comment.

MAX: But you don't just stay in bed? What do you do?

MARION: Sometimes I do, but rarely. I think to fully 'just be' you have to get out of bed at least. If only to give it the full body experience.

MAX: Any time constraints on that?

MARION: None whatsoever. I get up when I've slept enough.

MAX: So describe this nothing you do all day.

MARION: What after I get up?

MAX: Yes. Unless that exhausts the exciting, action packed part.

MARION: I eat something for breakfast. I go for a run. I do what I like until lunch. Then I eat lunch. After lunch I go for a walk and then let the rest of the day take care of itself.

MAX: Don't forget dinner.

MARION: I don't forget dinner.

MAX: And after dinner?

MARION: Sometimes I watch television.

MAX: Shocking. Are you doing any work?

MARION: I have done. But, although I'm on call, the phone rarely rings. Funny isn't it? I have thirty years of experience at the topmost level of education, I'm virtually offering to give it away, and no one seems to have the slightest interest. Or, what is more disturbing, the slightest need.

MAX: What do you do for money?

MARION: My needs are very few. I have enough to live on.

SCENE 4

MAX: Do you see anyone?

MARION: I'm rushed off my feet. Last week two of my friends wanted to meet me for coffee.

MAX: Chaos. And what about sex?

MARION: What about sex?

MAX: What do you do about it?

MARION: Not very much. I hooked up with one woman online, but it all started to get a bit too much like a commitment.

MAX: You mean she wanted a relationship?

MARION: I don't know. I was really busy with all the coffee dates so I didn't show up in the end.

MAX: Mmm, a real shag-fest. And what about love?

MARION: Love? I have had that from my friends and family and it does not come without obligation. 'On my terms' doesn't exist when anyone else is involved.

MAX: I can't believe you are happy.

MARION: Can't you? I'm sure you could if you thought about it a bit.

MARION gets busy with a book.

MAX: *[Sits and addresses the audience]* So, I left her there. There was nothing I could really do for Marion. She said she was happy. I did think about it a bit, but I still couldn't believe it. What can you do for someone who wants to be nothing? Or thinks she does. Then again perhaps she's right. Perhaps it is best to leave people to their illusions. Even if they are comparatively quiet and sedate when illusions are usually so noisy and bombastic. That's what Marion is – the silent illusionist.

End Scene.

ENTR'ACTE

MAX (SINGS)

Hello darling, how are you,
I heard you had some trouble?
Mild depression, home repossession,
That inner-city bubble.
Did I tell you, my cat went missing?
I don't know what I'll do.
I'm trying hard to make this sound like conversation
But in the end, it's really just about me.
Hey, you kids there, what are you doing
Having all that screen time?
Do your homework, competitive sport
Prompt attendance at family mealtimes.
    When I was nearly your age
    I managed to have fun too.
I'm trying to make, this story sound, like condemnation,
But in the end, it's really just about me.
Have you read the news today?
The story about migration?
Right-wing polis, speaking out
A source of consternation.
    Actually, I knew one well
    He was in my house at school.
I'm trying to say something profound about One Nation
But in the end, it's really just about me.
I say something, you say something
I pretend some fascination.
I'm really hearing nothing? you say.
Conservation masturbation.
    Round and round and round it goes,
    The tedium never ends.
I'm pretty sure, it's nothing more th'an hallucination
And in the end, it's really just about me.

End Entr'Acte.

SCENE FIVE

MARION is at home, madly running on a treadmill and pumping weights.

MARION: *[On treadmill]* Oh, hello darling.

MAX: *[Rushing in]* Is it true?

MARION: What?

MAX: That reference you gave me. I've just got off the phone from someone at the school and they pretty much told me that when my name came up for that job, you shat all over me.

MARION: I wouldn't put it that way.

MAX: How would you put it?

MARION: I simply pointed out that you are not particularly good at keeping focus and that you are not exactly leadership material.

MAX: What?

MARION: Don't worry. I said all sorts of positive things about you, of course. I couldn't make it all jam – they all know we've been friends for years.

MAX: Marion, it's private piano lessons, I don't really see where focus or leadership capacity come into it. I'm not applying to run the cadet corps or direct the school musical.

MARION: Cadets at an all-girl school. That's a stimulating thought. Frankly, I don't think it is a good idea that we work together anyway.

MAX: I didn't even know you were there anymore. Last time we spoke I thought you were closer to joining some sort of ascetic desert community than returning to school.

MARION: And how long ago was that?

MAX: I don't know. About a year ago?

MARION: That's focus.

MAX: What? Are you questioning my consistency because I never organise a coffee catch-up.

MARION: No, that's leadership capacity.

MAX: For goodness sake. You're sure you're not confusing your feelings about me as a friend with your feelings about me as musician.

MARION: The music school wants a professional facilitator, not a musician. Anyway I don't mind your inconsistency and lack of initiative as a friend. But as a colleague, it could become annoying.

MAX: Fuck you Marion. I'll never get that job now.

MARION: I know. I just gave it to Ellen Billings.

MAX: What? You did? Since when has it been up to you?

MARION: Since I took over as head of school.

MAX: When was that?

MARION: About six months ago.

MAX: You never told me about it.

MARION: You never asked! Look, don't worry about the job. They need oboe at a whole bunch of schools that don't give two hoots about KPIs and PSIs and RSIs, I'll recommend you and you'll be in a job in a week.

MAX: Well, you might have saved me a lot of stress if you had told me you felt that way.

MARION: Stress is good for you. Stimulates your creativity.

MAX: My creativity? Now you are just being insulting.

MARION: And your inner drive.

MAX: My inner drive? What's happened to you?

MARION: Nothing very much. I have just brought about a bit of a change of pace.

MAX: And when did this happen? Last time I saw you, albeit a year ago, you seemed to be pretty hard pressed to make it out of bed. And I did try to arrange several catch-ups with you, by the way. If you look at your text feed you will see it all. Frankly, it seemed to me that coffee and cake at Babka was somewhat pressing on your busy schedule of sitting on the couch all day and meditating.

MARION: You may have something there.

MAX: So, what did happen?

MARION: One day I woke up and said to myself "this is ridiculous". I had a shower, got dressed, drove into school and plonked myself down at my usual desk.

MAX: Are you mad? What did everyone say?

MARION: It was pretty bold, I admit. But no one said anything about it. Stacy, you know, been there since the flood, simply rolled her eyes at me in a sympathetic way. The Millennials on staff asked me how my holidays were and the head's PA – my PA now – snapped at me in the staff room and said rather sarcastically that it would be nice if, before the kids arrived back next year, she had some semblance of my teaching plan.

MAX: Didn't they know that you had resigned?

MARION: Apparently not. They might have thought I was on leave. Or, it did cross my mind, they might have thought I was on 'stress leave' and were just too polite to mention it.

MAX: Well the head must have known. I mean the ex-head.

SCENE 5

MARION: That's just it. She obviously didn't know what was going on. If she did know that I had resigned, she must have thought she buggered up the paperwork or something and just carried on as if nothing was out of the ordinary. That's when I knew she was losing it.

MAX: And you could swoop in.

MARION: Sort of.

MAX: Sounds like a madhouse. Perhaps it is best I don't work there.

MARION: *[Smiling]* I knew you would see it my way.

MAX: You don't think it might be best to move on yourself and find somewhere a little less weird?

MARION: I did think that but then I thought that it's probably just as mad everywhere else so I might as well make the best of it. So now I really am the idiot who has taken over the asylum.

MAX: And how did you manage that?

MARION: Superbly. I simply took all the stress and rudeness and calculating behaviour that most people save for their domestic sphere and transferred it to the workplace where it really belongs.

MAX: Oh really? And what exactly did that involve?

MARION: Utter disruption.

MAX: That sounds exhausting.

MARION: It is at first. Then you really get high on it. It gives you the most incredible feeling.

MAX: And how exactly do you manage this non-synthetic buzz. It is non-synthetic?

MARION: Totally. You just pursue, aggressively, all the inclinations that are completely at odds with your usual behaviour. You take all the politeness and consideration, altruism, collegiality, charm, warmth and humour and you chuck 'em out and do the exact opposite. Tantrums, obstruction, petty deceit, selfishness, mind games, braggadocio, one-upmanship – all these become your weapons of choice. If anyone ever asks you, "Do you think this kind of behaviour is appropriate in the workplace?", or even thinks it, the answer is "You bet it is!" If you ever stop yourself and think 'Am I carrying on in a completely unreasonable, narcissistic and childish way?' You know then you are onto something.

MAX: Sounds completely insecure.

MARION: But that is it! That is absolutely it! Complete insecurity is when you have utterly sealed the deal. That's what Shakespeare meant, "Security is mortals' chiefest enemy", I know it.

MAX: I doubt Old Bill was attempting to instruct the office arsehole.

SCENE 5

MARION: Don't you be too sure. He was probably a real shit at the Fabian Society. Constantly bragging about his latest play and telling everyone how cool it was to be a vegetarian or how awesome he looked in his Dr Jaeger stockinette suit.

MAX: So, is that what you did?

MARION: Pretty much. I kicked off by telling the boss she looked tired, warned one or two of the younger members of staff not to fraternise with the parents and started madly sucking up to, or insulting, various members of the school council and it all largely fell into place from there.

MAX: And you are managing to keep this up?

MARION: Yeah, I told you. It's highly addictive. It really is the easiest thing in the world and I am thoroughly enjoying myself.

MAX: So long as you know when to turn it off? What do Alex and the kids think of all this?

MARION: Of course I do. That's the point. Most of us save all our civilised inclinations for workplaces that treat us like shit and then we come home an unleash the horrible Id on our poor, underserving families. We are all mad, going on like that. It's fundamentally the opposite of what we should be doing.

MAX: So that's the way Alex sees it.

MARION: She's back, isn't she? And the kids too. Our place is now an oasis of reasonable, ideal living. We've become more polite to each other, we're supportive, we enjoy each other's company. We don't have to go to New York for all this, it's right here in St Louis. Right here in our own town!

MAX: Oh God, the gospel according to Louis B Mayer.

MARION: *[Sings]* "Don't tell me the lights are shining, any place but there."

MAX: But all that aggro, can't be good for you? All the stress of having to be rude to people every day, not forgetting the little insulting remark, starting bush fires everywhere and creating major problems out of the minutest and most insignificant things. Do you really want to be that person? Wouldn't it simply be easier to be your usual, sympathetic self?

MARION: That's where all our problems begin. Keep all that sympathy and empathy for home, I say. Save it for those for whom it will do most good. And those who appreciate it.

MAX: And let everyone at work get all the 'kick the dog' stuff.

MARION: Metaphorically, yes. It really is the best plan. I can't exaggerate how enjoyable it really is. Not to mention how successful I have found it.

MAX: Yes. You certainly do seem much happier. You seem to have acquired a kind of glow. An aura. I can't quite describe what has come over you. It's frightening, but... yes... you are right. There's something quite magnetic about you in this state. You are like some sort of glowing, radiant, new Millennial Machiavelli. You don't mind me saying that?

MARION: Not at all.

MAX: But that is it, you know. I know what you are now. You're the gay disruptor.

MARION: You're right. That's exactly what I am.

MAX: And disruption is quite obviously the key to happiness.

MARION: Quite obviously. Crazy isn't it.

Curtain.

www.ingramcontent.com/pod-product-compliance
Lightning Source LLC
Chambersburg PA
CBHW071322080526
44587CB00018B/3318